The Moon

Earth's Satellite

By Daisy Allyn

Gareth Stevens
Publishing

Please visit our Web site, www.garethstevens.com. For a free color catalog of all our high-quality books, call toll free 1-800-542-2595 or fax 1-877-542-2596.

Library of Congress Cataloging-in-Publication Data

Allyn, Daisy.
The moon : earth's satellite / Daisy Allyn.
    p. cm. — (Our solar system)
Includes index.
ISBN 978-1-4339-3831-3 (pbk.)
ISBN 978-1-4339-3832-0 (6 pack)
ISBN 978-1-4339-3830-6 (library binding)
1. Moon—Juvenile literature. I. Title.
QB582.A55 2011
523.3—dc22
                                            2010012653

First Edition

Published in 2011 by
Gareth Stevens Publishing
111 East 14th Street, Suite 349
New York, NY 10003

Designer: Daniel Hosek
Editor: Greg Roza

Photo credits: Cover, pp. 1, 7 (both), 11, 13, 21, back cover © Photodisc; pp. 5, 15, 17, 19 Shutterstock.com; p. 9 NASA/Getty Images.

Printed in the United States of America

CPSIA compliance information: Batch #CS10GS: For further information contact Gareth Stevens, New York, New York at 1-800-542-2595.

Contents

Boldface words appear in the glossary.

What Is a Moon?

A moon is like a little planet. Moons **orbit** planets, just as the planets of our **solar system** orbit the sun. Moons are also called satellites.

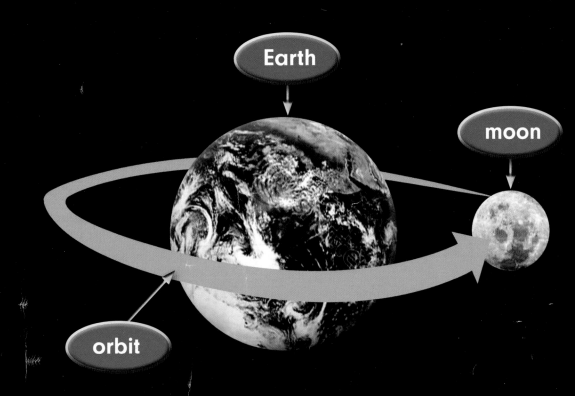

Earth

moon

orbit

5

Earth's Moon

Earth has one moon. The moon is about $\frac{1}{4}$ as wide as Earth. It would take more than 2 weeks to fly there in a fast jet!

On the Moon

On the moon, the sky always looks black. This is because there is very little air around the moon. Plants, animals, and people would not be able to live on the moon.

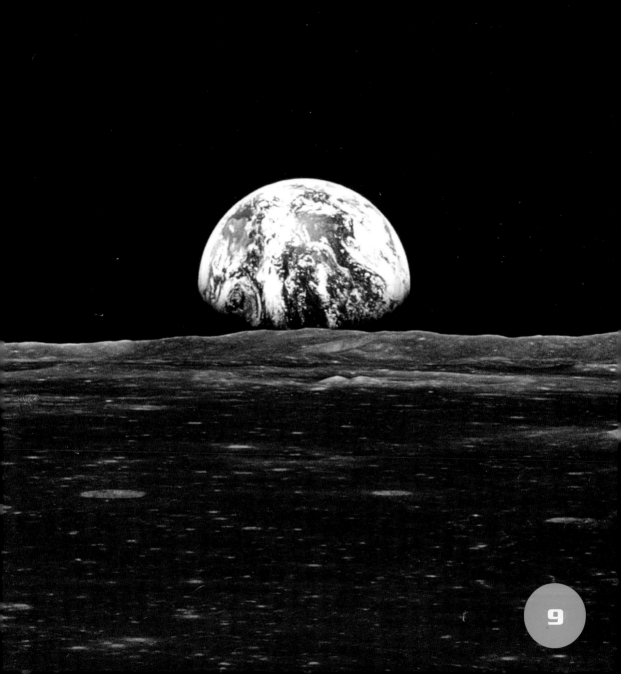

The moon's **surface** is covered with rocks and dust. It has lowlands, which look dark. It also has highlands, which look white.

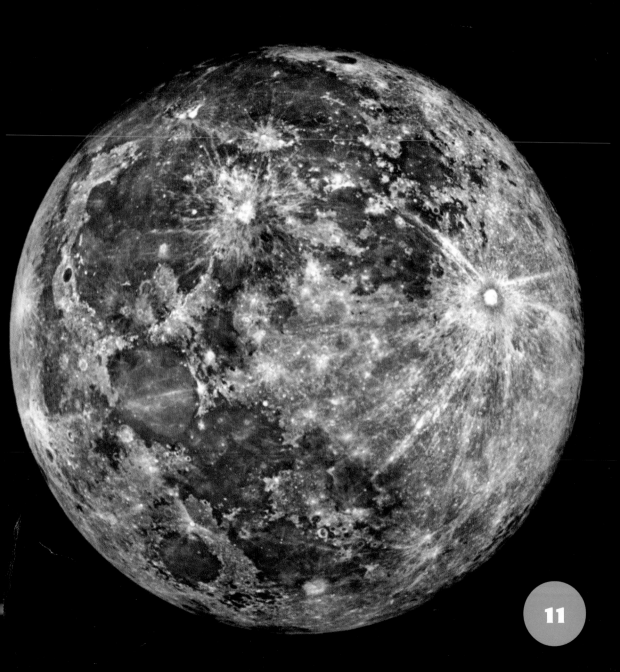

The moon has many **craters**. They were made when space rocks crashed into the moon long ago.

The Changing Moon

The moon does not make its own light. We see it because sunlight hits it and shines off it.

The moon seems to change shape. That is because the amount of the lighted side that we can see changes. These different views are called phases.

phases of the moon

17

Earth's Tides

The moon's **gravity** pulls on Earth's oceans and creates tides. Tides are the regular rise and fall of water levels in the oceans.

People on the Moon

In 1969, American **astronauts** landed on the moon. They even walked on the moon's surface! Many people want to send astronauts back to the moon someday.

Glossary

astronaut: someone who works or lives in space

crater: a bowl-shaped hole on the surface of a planet or moon

gravity: the force that pulls objects toward the center of a planet or moon

orbit: to travel in a circle or oval around something

solar system: the sun and all the space objects that orbit it, including the planets and their moons

surface: the top part of a planet or moon; the ground

For More Information

Books

Eckart, Edana. *Watching the Moon*. New York, NY: Children's Press, 2004.

Olson, Gillia M. *Phases of the Moon*. Mankato, MN: Capstone Press, 2007.

Web Sites

Earth's Moon

www.kidsastronomy.com/earth/moons.htm
Read facts about Earth's moon and find links to other planets and moons in our solar system.

Quiz Your Noodle: The Moon

kids.nationalgeographic.com/Games/PuzzlesQuizzes/
Quizyournoodle-the-moon
Take a quiz about the moon.

Index

About the Author

Daisy Allyn teaches chemistry and physics at a small high school in western New York. A science teacher by day, Allyn spends many nights with her telescope, exploring the solar system. Her Great Dane, Titan, often joins Allyn on her nightly star-gazing missions.